BOY;
MEN DON'T CRY

By

Gilbert Bent

To the men and boys who will become men and their households that will nurture them along their journey. The future depends on your success, so take your time to listen, grow, and love.

Life is what you make it.

Acknowledgment

First, let me give all the thanks and praise to GOD; without Him, nothing is possible. I want to acknowledge the struggles in life that give us an appreciation for our successes. Thank you to my mother and deceased father, who made my life possible. I greatly appreciate my children, who made my life purposeful, striving for a better life for them than I had.

Thanks to my siblings, who are always available, these are the bonds that keep the family together. Thanks to my friends and all the reasoning sessions. Thanks to my mentors and professional colleagues, I have gained knowledge and a perspective to be forever grateful. Special thanks to my fiancé Janelle Callender; it was destiny by chance. Thanks to Paradox Unlimited Company.

Table of Contents

Introduction

"Come on, man up, dude!"

"Be a man!"

"You can't cry; you are a man!"

***

How often do we hear such statements where a man's masculinity is questioned because of his actions or the lack thereof?

Gender stereotypes often portray women as sensitive and mawkish while men are generally portrayed as the stronghold, a foundation, a pillar of some sort, standing tall and protecting his dependents. Somehow, people have mostly looked upon men as the strong, tough exterior that can withstand any adversity.

Men generally are not at liberty to express their emotions. Any kind of negative emotion, such as sadness in particular, if shown by the shedding of a tear or two is considered unmanly. Thus, a man expresses his negative emotions as anger, which is more societally acceptable than a man crying out of grief or remorse. Anger, either bottled up or ranted out eventually leads to aggression. Aggression, therefore, becomes an integral part of the masculine persona.

It is this aggression in a man that results in personal, or job-related tensions that may eventually progress into the labelling of men as insensitive.

Men are also expected to be naturally dominant.

It is a personality trait that they develop during the juvenile stages of life. Young boys are raised, with a mind-set of being superior. When a male child matures into a teenager, he starts exerting a certain level of dominance and superiority over women (or the less dominant, obedient ones) he finds himself surrounded by and interacting with. This begins their transition from an obedient child to an assertive, commanding and controlling man.

It has also been witnessed that any young boy who does not show traits of dominance, superiority or aggression is laughed upon, made fun of and sometimes even bullied by his fellows until he can't endure it anymore and fights back against his abusers. If he does not develop enough courage to stand up against his bullies, he develops a mechanism of taking out his frustration on people who are weaker than him. This again leads to a man becoming aggressive and violent transforming the boy into someone that could be deemed manly by society.

The rough and tough exterior of a man's body only adds fuel to the fire. The muscle bulk and the increased physical strength as compared to a woman, make men look and feel powerful. This makes them think that they can conquer anything just by using the strength of their body. Sometimes, this even leads to them abusing those who are not as strong.

Violence is often associated with men.

Although throughout history there are countless accounts of men being violent, it is still not a trait that is solely attached to them. Women too have shown this trait and sometimes are even worse than men when it comes to displaying it. Nevertheless, men are generally considered to be tough, insensitive beings and sometimes exhibit violence.

The violent streak in men is also perhaps the reason for the many wars that the world has seen throughout history. A deadly combination of physical strength, power, and egoistical thinking in a man not only leads to an argument breaking out but also leads to wars. This takes away precious lives and ruins happy families specifically those who had no direct interest or reason to go to war other than the fact that it was ordered by those in authoritative positions.

Men are considered to be very egotistic.

As discussed, this ego is developed by their upbringing and leads men to believe that they could rule the world. Men then set out to conquer the world by force. Some use their intellect while others use weapons. Either way, the peace of the world is hindered by these measures and chaos erupts wherever these men decide to invade. This is not to say that woman have not been conquerors in history, it is only to emphasize that men are more prone to this trait.

In all the above-mentioned scenarios, if a man shows no interest in the given events and is not enthusiastic to follow in the footsteps of other men, it is looked upon by the society as amateurish. Such a man is then the odd one out and is on the verge of losing respect.

Not only that, it is also considered less manly if a man cries out for help. Men are supposed to be problem solvers. Failure to do so results in the man being labelled as incompetent. His gender identity is questioned and he is considered to be deficient of a characteristic male trait. He is often frowned upon. Who gets to decide that this problem-solving trait was only meant for males?

In all their superiority, men may start to think that they are better than their female counterparts. Men are considered to be more logical, practical and sensible. This often results in men abusing the females in their life by calling them names and thinking of them as foolish. They reckon that a female is less intelligent than them and is not capable of achieving what a man could. The opinion or suggestion of a woman becomes less valuable as compared to a man's, satisfying the man's ego.

Men are also considered practical, while women are emotional. So, in this regard a man always has to analyze the real perspectives while a woman's perspectives are dismissed as they are thought to stem from her emotions.

If a man feels emotional under any circumstances, he is supposed to hide it and bury it inside of him. A man who shows his emotions finds himself near the border of the manly hood circle and is almost thrown out of the circle if he does not start to act manly enough to be accepted by the society again.

In our everyday life we see how men boast about their manliness and are proud to be born as the male. Just having the physical characteristics of a male tends to give them the power to think they can do whatever they want without consequences. Men usually get their way when it comes to doing things and if questioned they reply that they are men and are at liberty to do as they please.

When in a relationship, men are generally allowed to be possessive about the woman they date or marry, while if the woman shows the same emotion, she is labelled as being insecure. Here again we see how men think it's okay for them to possess a woman as if she is an entity to acquire and keep. However, that freedom is not given to the woman.

When it comes to the matters of grief, men again are to hide their emotions and not cry. Men usually cry behind closed doors to let out their emotions for if anyone was to see them, they would question their masculinity and that may also lead to a man being ostracized for his decreased manliness.

On the contrary, women are allowed by society to express their emotions as they want to. Rather, if a woman doesn't express her emotions for whatever reason, her feminity is questioned.

It is an age-old unrealistic expectation and practice for society to separate the two genders enough to make them fit into a specific role. Women are to possess characteristics such as compassion so as to perform their designated task of bearing and rearing children as well as taking care of the household.

Men, on the other hand, are to be strong, tough, rational, practical, analytical and realistic so that they may go out of the house and be the breadwinner and take care of his dependents. This separation of the two genders causes men to be portrayed as something they are not. This is all a myth that has been passed down over generations while the truth has been hidden from us.

The separation of genders with respect to their gender identities, and their roles in society causes more harm than healing. It creates issues of inequality between men and women.

Human beings are vulnerable by nature.

Why then are men expected to hide their sensitive side?

Is it not natural to grieve upon the death of someone close?

If a man is abused, he too would feel the pain and trauma that a woman would experience under the same circumstances. Then why is he supposed to go about life as though nothing happened?

This is the inequality that men face in the world. It is clearly unjust and leads to aggression which is eventually taken out on the dependents of a man causing domestic problems.

Just because he is a man, he is expected to be the strong one in every situation. The one who does not crumble due to his feelings and the one who fights till his last breath. He is supposed to be in control at all times- a fearless and bold person. If he gives up too soon or does not stand up for himself or his family, then he is not man enough.

Women are allowed to feel, express, cry, and be vulnerable. If they fail to maintain their composure under a stressful situation, they will not be held accountable to the extent that a man would. Again, an identifiable inequality so obvious that the society cannot turn a blind eye to it.

The domestic issues that develop due to this amount of inequality also leads to a situation where a woman has to be strong and bold, or show her masculine side of being steadfast in difficult times. Here, the woman is questioned and the society disapproves of her as she is told that she has lost the very sense of feminity.

There have been times where the dominance and aggression of men has increased many folds, so much so that the women suffer at the hands of those she was to be protected by. If a man was allowed to express his emotions like a woman, then these issues would probably lessen.

Society's standards of masculinity for men and feminity for women can also cause the situation of domestic violence to flip. It is generally thought that an abuser would be a man and a victim would be a woman. This thought is based on society's idealization of a man being a certain way. However, this is not always the case.

Although men are physically strong, not all men use this difference to abuse their female dependents or partners. And women being equally intelligent as men can also manipulate the situation into playing the victim while herself being the abuser. In this situation, society tends to favor the woman just because it is difficult to comprehend that someone who is considered less strong and less smart, can use mental tactics to get favor from the masses.

The inequality caused by the separation of men and women as having masculine or feminine traits defining them leads to global tribulations. People have created certain perceptions in their minds pertaining to the two genders. It seems that if any of the two genders deviate slightly from what is considered to be their trait, the society is quick to judge and disapprove of that particular individual be it a man or a woman.

Although, it causes a lot of chaos in the world, society still does not want to see a change and is okay living with this false idealization.

Unfortunately, what we fail to realize is the fact that men and women were not created to be separated, rather they were made to complement each other.

The traits given to both genders were not finite and definite. Both genders have been given those traits in amounts required to complement each other. If a man is abused and feels taken advantage of, it should be okay for him to express his emotions of insecurity and hurt, without the fear of being judged by society of being any less of a man than anybody else.

In the same way, if a woman is undergoing a situation where she needs to be strong and stand up for herself then she should be able to do so without being afraid of any kind of bias consequences that she may endure later as a result of her standing her ground.

As human beings, we experience all sorts of emotions. Bottling them up inside of us just because we are to be labeled as a gentleman or a lady becomes harmful to our mental, emotional and physical wellbeing. Gender roles, and traits are only meant to identify man and woman as different, not to invite injustice. For example, gender stereotypes need not dictate that a man cannot stay at home and take care of the household or a woman cannot go out and work and be the breadwinner of the family.

A man can be sensitive, compassionate and considerate while also being strong, supportive, logical, a problem-solver and a protector. A woman can be strong minded, steadfast, level-headed while being her feminine self of grace, kindness, empathy, gentleness and sophistication.

Hence, it can be concluded that men are not what the society labels them to be. They are also human beings, with feelings and emotions and the need to express them when possible. It is completely unfair if one gender is permitted to show how they feel while the other has to suffer in silence just so that they can hold the macho man image created in the mind of people of society. It is this image of the man that has created innumerable issues that the world faces today. We are fighting for equality for women, ignoring the male side of the story.

Can we not accept both genders just as they are?

Complementary, NOT competitive.

Men and women need not be transformed by society. A world where men and women can be nothing but themselves is an ideal world. For even men need the comfort of a mother's warm embrace.

Chapter One: Blessed Man

12 September 1988.

It was a day like no other. Everything seemed out of sync. There was a mess everywhere. The sky changed from sunny to an overcast of dark apocalyptic clouds everywhere. Dust and leaves flew in every direction, and screams filled the air as people were swept away by the formidable winds. It was almost as though the whole world had turned upside down. The people of Jamaica were in for quite a stir. Amid all this, innocence was crushed as children witnessed death and destruction firsthand.

It's not easy for a child to cope with the concept of death; to see a loved one, or anyone for that matter, lying in a permanent state of unconsciousness. It's something even an adult cannot comprehend, let alone a child. This is the case with funerals; a child's mind does not understand that once a dead person is buried, they can never return. It is perhaps after a certain age, say five years, that a child achieves some understanding of the concept of death.

Until then, any signs of death and destruction are incomprehensible for children and hence cause panic and result in trauma or PTSD. The day all hell broke loose in Jamaica caused many children to suffer the same.

It was the same unfortunate day when a scared and whimpering four-year-old child stared out of his house as the window rattled ominously. I could see the street stretching out till afar, and the sight was not inviting. I watched in fear as the winds uprooted trees and people ran towards their houses in alarm. Back then, the roof of the standard homes in our community were made of Zinc (sheet metal), and you could hear the rain crashing like cymbals if the roof was not already taken away by the wind.

My mother took me in a warm embrace and said, "Gilbert! Let's make our way to the other side of the house, where there is a concrete slab for a roof." Her voice broke, unable to hide her emotions.

I can never forget that day. Not only the devastation it caused but also the name of the hurricane would forever be etched in my mind. After all, I shared my name with a storm so powerful that it wrecked havoc across Jamaica. Everything was upturned. Our lives changed for the worse in a matter of minutes. The houses across the Island were damaged, perhaps beyond repair. More than two hundred died, while nearly five hundred thousand were left homeless. And that was almost one-fourth of the Island's population at the time. Utter chaos and terror took over the land as people cried out for help.

Among them, my mother was one of the strongest and bravest individuals who managed to keep her wits. Although shook to the core, she had a plan — to save her family by sheltering on the side where the roof was made of a concrete slab. This part of the house was a recent addition. But the fear still lurked around us. What would happen if the house caved? The answer was clear and simple: We would be buried under all the rubble.

As we made our way to the other side of the house, the winds blew a door that struck my mom in her back. The Zinc roof of the house was also being peeled back by the force of the winds. Hurricane winds smashed the windows and caused the pedestrians to struggle to keep their feet on the ground. Almost every home was without electricity for days. The havoc was unbearable. With so much damage and loss, one only prayed for their life to be saved.

Nevertheless, such traumatic incidents have an odd way of bringing people together. That day we saved the lives of many others by sheltering them in our home as the storm had already taken their roof and belongings away. I remember being grateful to be surrounded by friends and family during such a crucial time.

Despite being a kid, merely four years old, I could comprehend the gravity of the situation. I knew we were up against a mighty calamity, and I sensed that it would take us a long time to resurface from the destruction the hurricane had caused. The infrastructure had been affected beyond one's imagination, and the government bodies would have a tough time bringing things back to normal as looting and crime became normal amidst the devastation. But these were things I didn't know as a child. All I knew and could see was that we were severely affected due to a very destructive and powerful storm.

So, in the wake of the hurricane, all I could do as a child was wait it out while the adults made arrangements to secure whatever they could and later rebuild our lives.

At that time, we had two homes in our rural community back in Jamaica. Both homes were on the same block, one belonging to my mother and one to her husband at the time. I clearly remember the devastation caused by the hurricane. It blew away people's roofs and injured many. The sight was heart-wrenching and even more frightening. We sheltered as many as we could in our house, including family and friends; whoever didn't have a roof or power took refuge in our home. While hiding on the other side of the house was necessary, we also knew that we had to risk our lives and take certain precautionary measures.

While taking these precautionary measures, I distinctly remember preparing before the storm came by using leftover cement blocks on the zinc roof to prevent the wind from blowing it away. This worked for a while until a strong gust of wind took that too. A portion of our other expansion had a slab concrete roof which we stayed in. In an attempt to make the most of a dire situation, we came together as a community, and that was the silver lining for me. I reiterate this because it brought together some of the friends that I have to this day. There is something surreal about the feeling of being able to provide support to our family and friends at that time.

After all, being able to help others is a blessing because it is as though God chose you to deliver comfort to a brother in

Christ. I felt as though my family and I were selected as an answer to the prayers for safety that people were desperately willing to be fulfilled. Nobody wants to die, of course, and in a storm like Hurricane Gilbert, when death is looming ever so close and fear is staring you right in the face, it is only then you realize who your savior is. Only then, the faces of those willing to stand by you and shelter you are unmasked.

Given that we were helping so many people, I remember feeling humbled by the whole situation. But since I was a kid, it impacted me that the hurricane and I shared the same name. Songs were written by various artists to depict the event, and, to this day, I still get teased because my name is Gilbert. The impact, however, was profound because I used to view that as a representation of who I am and what I could become. I felt I was capable of great things; while my aim was not death or destruction, I felt that being akin to a storm meant that I had inexhaustive energy that would enable me to scale great heights. To me, it also meant that I was unrelenting and highly determined to make my way through any blockages in the road of life. At the same time, I would look at my father as a person of authority, a person in a position of power. Gilbert Sr's stature made me believe that I, too, could follow in his footsteps and be someone of high acclaim.

Having the same name as the hurricane gave me a feeling of empowerment and passion. People, both young and old, would tell me that the fact that I shared the name of a hurricane was a sign that I would achieve greatness in life, and I guess, as an impressionable young boy, when people told me this, I believed them. I believed that I was going to be great, that I was going to be successful. It could mean being powerful and devastating, just like Hurricane Gilbert, yet it left an impression on me.

While Hurricane Gilbert was one of my most painful experiences, I would still say that growing up in Jamaica was the best time of my life. The place is rich in culture and food, and the vibe is different. As a young person, I used to go back and forth between different communities and was free to travel independently even at an early age. Although my mom and dad were separated, it didn't really impact me because I had two and sometimes three of everything. Two houses, two moms, two dads. It was very fulfilling to have so many people who love and watch out for you. Don't they say, the more, the merrier? I loved spending time with my father the most among all my family members.

My father was a man who commanded respect. He was a police officer in the Jamaica Constabulary Force, rose to the ranks of a detective, held many different positions within the forces, and trained many people. He was a very respectable officer and a very stern disciplinarian. You might say he is indelible. However, he was very kind-hearted and lovable if you got to know him.

My mother, on the other hand, was a tough lover. She was very kind but had very high expectations for her children. More than that, she always knew what she liked and would expect others to live up to her expectations. She had a secondary school education, but she did many different jobs. She served as a records clerk and secretary at the Ministry of Health.

Despite having just secondary education, one could never tell because she carried herself so well. She took good care of her kids and raised us well. She always chose the best for us and, in retrospect, she succeeded. She put the house together with the best furniture she could afford and cleaned and maintained it as best as she could. My mother thought I was lucky as she had contemplated not carrying me to full term due to being in an abusive relationship with my father at the time. He begged her to keep me and she conceded, hoping he would change.

She was always a very hard-working woman, and sacrifice came as part and parcel of it. She had to travel a lot, and we would be left with what you would call 'guardians,' 'sitters,' or 'custodians' from time to time. That's how growing up was for me. A mother who cares for her children must make difficult life choices. She can either choose to stay home and nurture her children personally or go out to work to earn the bread and forgo the opportunity to be there with her children.

My mother and father chose to do the latter, which meant that we spent a lot of time with people who were not related to us and may not have had our best interests at heart. In my view, there are many downsides to handing your children over to caretakers. The child may not be comfortable with the caretaker as some children are shy and introverted, as I was.

Caretakers could become verbally or physically abusive towards the child, ruining their self-esteem and demoralizing the child. Some are even not capable of nurturing your young one's minds as children need mental stimulation, love, and support. It is necessary to ensure the peace of mind of one's child, but sometimes parents have to make such decisions.

After all, it is only if they earn well that parents will be able to put food on the table and afford a good education for their child.

My parents were no different. They worked very hard to achieve their dreams and provide us with the best opportunities. At a young age, I traveled a lot which was rare for people back then. Traveling and getting your visa to travel abroad was a big thing in those days. However, such opportunities were frequently available to us.

I remember traveling and visiting my cousins in Brooklyn and family in Queens and The Bronx. I am lucky to have had such experiences. These experiences were more educational than bookish. I got to see the world firsthand and understand it from the perspective of a person who has witnessed and experienced many different cultures.

I was also lucky to spend quality time with my friends and teachers at school. A few things that really made a difference in my life were going out and indulging in different activities. One of my favorite teachers, Miss Shepard, profoundly touched my life. I believe she transformed many lives because of how caring she was. She showed us, students, a different side of life. She took us on a class trip to broaden our mindsets, and we were exposed to different communities where we realized we were one amongst a million. I consider myself to have had a blessed life. I had exposure to a lot of things. I didn't live with my father, but because I had that freedom, I had multiple homes to go to. I would only see my father sometimes on the weekends. He'd pick me up every weekend, and we would take a ride out to the country.

On our way back, he would stop and buy everybody drinks. My father had land and a farm out in the country, so traveling every weekend, paying homage, and giving back to the rural community was quite an experience. My father would take these times to teach me to drive, hunt and shoot, etc. These are such fond memories that I believe I could drive down that road with my eyes closed and still be able to identify and reach the place so well. Certainly, some things don't change.

Despite having so many fond memories, it's not as though my life was devoid of problems. Being the middle child and a rather quiet and shy person, I found myself crying if anyone spoke to me too harshly. If someone were to ask me to do something or give me a directive, I wouldn't respond, even if it was a playful one. I would only realize that I had been spoken to too harshly, and it would result in a bout of tears. It was that simple to make me cry.

I know I was a quiet and observant child. Being the middle child, I was spoiled, I would get away with things until I wasn't young enough to get away with them anymore. Middle children are often most neglected as the eldest, being the firstborn, holds a special place in parents' hearts, while the youngest gets the most love by virtue of being the endearing baby of the house. As far as getting away with things was concerned, I believe I got away with things because I often went unnoticed. When I grew old enough not to get away with something, I had difficulty or got into trouble. I would hide it; I wouldn't say anything to anybody. I would deal with it in my own way because I didn't want anybody to speak to me. So, I would just internalize things.

I remember one time, while walking to school, a dog bit me. My mother was out of the country on vacation, and our guardians were available. But because a guardian was not paying attention to me at that time, I covered it up. I left that dog bite as is for weeks and weeks until it started oozing with puss. I almost got gangrene, and I could have lost my leg. They realized when it began to smell.

Eventually, I was taken to the hospital for treatment. I am relating this incident to impress upon, the reader, the extent to which I was shy, reserved, and quiet. I would never speak unless spoken to. I think I covered stuff up because it wasn't my mother or father who was around. I did not have that comfort level with the caregiver to be able to tell them that I was injured, or maybe I did not want to expose my vulnerability in front of a stranger. All I wanted was to go unnoticed by the caregiver because I was too shy to be seen.

I had brothers and sisters I could talk to, but they were always busy with their own affairs. I felt that our caretaker, was sometimes abusive. Therefore, I was never vocal about issues that affected me in my childhood.

Despite not being so vocal, I was always self-motivated. My motivation was just to survive, make it to the other side, and be independent enough. I believe I did feel the need to be more vocal to address matters head-on. However, as a child, I felt that I just wanted to survive, to be seen and not heard.

I believe that to survive, we need to take the good with the bad and just live through our circumstances. Through all that time, I just think I held on to that. I believe I will be great; I will be the Gilbert that will be a force to be reckoned with. I told myself that I would do things differently when I got the opportunity. I always held on to my friends, who supported me through everything I went through. At the end of the day, I just look at those moments as painful experiences that I just had to get through and not let them affect me so that I could be a functional person.

That's how I dealt with all that happened to me. My parents eventually divorced, and I was elated to have access to so many things but never understood what I was missing. I was content to have the freedom but never realized that I was missing guidance in life.

I feel that every child needs to have someone to look up to - someone who inspires them and guides them. There is a profound impact on a child's life with the right guidance and attention. With a watchful guardian, will be of a stronger character. He would be able to understand the virtues of helping others and being honest and truthful. He would be bold and fearless in the face of life's struggles and have a well-nourished mind, body, and soul. Nonetheless, my parents raised me well, and I feel I am a blessed man.

Chapter Two: Am I Abused?

It often happens that children of divorced parents are sexually abused by strangers. Why is that so? I believe it happens because children from broken families are more vulnerable and susceptible to being misled. Furthermore, such children tend to crave love and attention from outsiders more than children with strong family backgrounds.

Now, my parents got divorced when I was really young. I don't know for sure the reasons or the difficulties that they faced which led to divorce. As a child, even before my parent's divorce, I found that we were moving around a lot, living with various aunts and uncles. I never really understood why.

I also have vague memories of my parents having confrontational arguments. My older sister was exposed to that environment much longer than I did, and she can vividly remember the details. Furthermore, my mother would frequently tell stories of being physically abused by my father being that he was an alcoholic. He would become violent after consuming alcohol soon after returning from work. As per my mother, the littlest things upset my father.

So that is a brief description of the household I grew up in for the initial few years of my life. My mother just couldn't go on living like that. Eventually, I grew up in a separate household, and my mother remarried, so I had a stepfather and stepsiblings. It was a very dynamic environment to grow up in. However, I never realized how growing up in such an environment tends to affect one's mental health.

Based on my experiences as a child, I was sure of one thing, I did not want to grow up to be like my father. I did not want to be physically abusive toward my partner. Knowing the kind of difficulties my mother had been through and the problem my father had with regard to controlling his temper, I found that living in that environment impacted my view of relationships and how I dealt with them.

I also came to know from my mother that initially, she did not want to disclose her whereabouts to my father because of his anger management issues, but eventually, when she settled down and both my parents had moved on in life, she encouraged my father to foster a good relationship with me.

I feel this was extremely important.

At that stage, I was not aware of why my parents lived in a separate house nor of the abuse my mother had been through. It was all disclosed to me at a later stage. So, I perceived my father as an important and respectable figure. After all, he was a policeman. I saw him as a hero. He would pick me up for the weekends, and we would go on trips. I learned a lot from him. One of the experiences I've loved was when he would take me hunting. I value these experiences with him, and the memories are still vivid in my mind.

So, on one hand, my childhood was traumatic, while on the other hand, I have some great memories to cherish.

I have wonderful memories with my father, but I find a very strong woman in my mother. Especially because she, as a single mother, took the decision to leave the island and migrate to the Americas in search of providing us with a life of better quality. When people get the opportunity to migrate to different countries; it's an opportunity that they won't just forego; it is, after all, an opportunity to make a better life for their family and loved ones.

So, when my mom got her opportunity, she left in order to ensure the best for us. During the summers, we would travel quite a lot, and I realized that it was a benefit and a privilege to be traveling at such a young age.

Nevertheless, for the majority of the school year, we were left with our caregivers. This put us in a tricky situation because these caregivers were not certified, and everybody has their way of giving care. For example, when my mother would send supplies, one of the caregivers would provide all supplies to her son and family. This was something I couldn't do much about, so I just let it pass. After all, I would soon be reunited with my mother, and that's all that mattered to me.

Eventually, I moved to the Americas. Education was always important to me and my family. I can remember going to one of the better schools in my community due to my mom pushing me. I studied at St. Catherine's Prep School. and finally graduated from one of the better high schools in that same area, St. Jago High.

From back in my school days, I have always been a friendly and charming person. Females found me exceptionally handsome and I had a good rapport with the females I liked and who liked me. I used to play sports and took part in all the interesting activities. My friends respected me, especially the ones who understood that I had a low tolerance for bullshit.

Coming back to how children of divorced parents are frequently abused. During the time that my mom had gone to the States, I faced various instances of physical abuse. For example, if I would go out and play and stay a little too late, then upon returning home, I'd get a beating. If I came home dirty with stains on my clothes, I'd get a beating. The expectations impressed on any children confused me.

I wasn't only mistreated in terms of physical abuse. I also experienced what I later realized was a clear case of sexual abuse.

I do not have a very vivid memory of the first time I was abused by my guardian at the time. I was perhaps about 9 or 10 years old and still resided at my mom's house.

One night I awakened from my sleep, suddenly feeling my hand being guided by someone. I was only semi-conscious, yet I distinctly remember touching something soft and squishy with a semi-hard roundness at the top. Furthermore, I clearly remember my hands slowly being moved down past her belly. My hands approached the area between her legs which was warm and wet. She also rubbed my penis gently, which got very hard. For some reason, I did not resist this so-called assault; I simply laid there, pretending to be asleep.

The next day, I let on as though nothing had happened the previous night. I simply got ready for school and waited for my uncle to drop off my siblings and me. This instance was repeated a couple more times in a similar fashion. I don't know why I never said anything. I didn't tell anyone, not even my friends at the time. Was it because I was afraid? Or was it because I found the experiences pleasurable and didn't want them to stop? I don't remember, as the decision not to tell anyone was not a conscious or conscientious one.

Fast forward two or three years, we had moved across the street to my stepdad's house. It was my freshman year in high school. We still lived in Jamaica. One night I once again awakened to the same experience where I would feel my hand moving and rubbing these soft and squishy breasts while my penis was being rubbed gently. However, this time around, I found myself being led to the front room where no one slept (that was my parents' room, and both were in America, so we kept the room clear and clean). That was where I was sometimes made to lay on the floor, and she would ride me until I felt a rush of sensation throughout my body, and my penis exploded. I had never felt this sensation before, but it felt good, oh so very good to me. I began to think that this is what a man is supposed to do.

Up until now, I did not tell anybody what was happening at this point, not even my friends. That quickly changed when one afternoon, after a game of football (soccer), all the boys sat around and talked about their sexual exploits. They prided themselves on the number of girlfriends they had. They spoke about sex and the conquest of a woman like it was a rite of passage. As it was, in Jamaican culture, if you didn't like women, then something was definitely wrong with you. In some cases, when they would offer to help you lose your virginity, they would say things like, "I will buss you on a big woman," and if the offer were accepted, they definitely would.

Later on, as my group of friends and I walked home, we continued the same conversation, and I decided to divulge my sexual experiences. So, I told my friends that my guardian had ridden my dick the previous night. At first, they looked shocked, as though they didn't believe me, but they then started to treat me as though I had won a gold medal. They encouraged me to keep up the game with my guardian. At that moment, any reservations or unpleasant feelings that I had were eased.

Life went on as normal.

Soon I grew bold. On one occasion, I arose in the middle of the night and went to her room. I started to feel her breasts, and by this time, I had already graduated to kissing and rubbing them. I fingered her vagina. Basically, I took the lead. I took her into the empty room and laid down on my back. I let her ride my penis as I heard the imaginary applause of all my friends.

My friends had convinced and comforted me into believing that my guardian and I were indeed having sex. Sometimes it became quite regular. I was now a teen and was somewhat proud of the fact that I was doing what all teen boys did. However, I did feel that I was not making time for girls my age. In high school, I did have girlfriends whom I claimed as my own, but I remember that I would never try to get them to have sex unless they pushed the issue because I knew if I wanted to, I could have sex at home. It was as though I had a backup plan.

Later in my adult life, when I was in America, I learned about the standards and laws surrounding child development and child abuse. Verbal or nonverbal consent is extremely important, and indulging in sexual acts with a minor is not only molestation and abuse but is a criminal act punishable by law. Suddenly, a light bulb went off in my head. I thought back to my early sexual experiences and wondered if I had been a willing participant. Or if I had been abused?

Chapter Three: Upping the Stakes

Jamaica was and always will be home. Home is not the place where you live. As they say, home is where the heart is, and my heart will forever be in Jamaica. For me, leaving Jamaica for the States was akin to being ruthlessly uprooted from my homeland. I did not take kindly to the move. After all, I was leaving behind my school friends, girlfriends, and team with whom I ran in the streets.

My reluctance to move delayed my immigration process. I was only 12 years old when we moved to the U.S, which is a very vulnerable age. An age at which the foundation of your personality is being laid. It could be said that these formative years or events that take place at this stage in your life are your defining moments. The move was quite an emotional experience for me. Leaving behind everything familiar made me feel as though one chapter of my life had ended while another had begun.

The major difference in my life after the move was that it was full of the unknown, which made me very anxious. I had traveled to the States before, but living there was a totally different ball game. Acclimatizing to a new environment and school, meeting new people, making new friends, and becoming aware of new surroundings and the locality we lived in… were all so challenging. When we moved to the U.S., the first place we lived in was East New York, Brooklyn. We lived in a basement on Miller Avenue before we got an apartment on Dumont Avenue. Somehow the biggest challenge in all of this was finding where I fit in.

It was difficult adjusting to the fast pace of life in the U.S. Not knowing how the system works or how to access it made it a harrowing experience for me. I would frequently get lost in the subway and on buses. Sometimes I would end up in other localities of the city. I was quick to learn that different boroughs of the city had different unwritten rules. Another element that made it difficult for me to adjust was how rude random people could be. As they rushed to their destinations, they would push you aside indifferently and tell you to get out of the way.

A challenge that proved to be a constant was overcoming the stereotypes that were associated with being Jamaican. The top four that always came to Americans' minds were that 'Jamaicans love to party and have fun,' 'Jamaicans don't love to work/hustle,' or 'all Jamaicans are very aggressive and violent' and 'everybody from Jamaica loves to smoke weed.' Now that I think about it, we are so much more than that, but if the general public continues to stereotype you, it is indeed the most imposing form of peer pressure. One begins to conform in some way or the other in order to fit in with the local crowd, be it culture driven or in terms of circumstances.

As aforesaid, another challenge was that when the family first moved to the States, we lived in my stepdad's family's basement on Miller Avenue. I had a good relationship with his family but was still uncomfortable because I missed my home so much. I used to sleep next to the boiler on a small twin bed.

I remember thinking, "Was this what I had left my bed and my home in Jamaica for?" It was not as though I had a choice in the matter anyway, so I just had to make the most of what life had to offer at that point. The child in me took it as an adventure. I began to get used to the sound of the ice cream trucks pulling up to the house and learning how to play Double Dutch on the street. I remember that on hot days every other block turned on the fire hydrant, and there was a street waterpark. Our first summer in the States passed quickly, and we then moved to a two-bedroom apartment on Dumont Avenue. My siblings and I shared a room. It was better, but I was still on a twin bed.

I remember my mom telling me that she was looking forward to me beginning high school in a couple of days, and I asked her which school I would attend. We had visited a few, and she was to decide. She replied, "The one in Canarsie," and continued to say, "Just take the B6 bus and get off at Rockaway."

I was surprised she said it so casually, as though I knew or understood anything she just said. I asked her to take me on a quick practice run, and I was lucky she did. Otherwise, I would have gotten lost.

An odd memory from my first day of school was that I got a big surprise while traveling to school alone. On the way, the bus passed a bunch of naked women walking all over the street and blocking the traffic. I had never seen such a sight, that out in the open, before. I thought that America itself was a great school. Look at what I had witnessed, and I hadn't even reached school as yet. I reached school pretty excited, but that excitement soon died as I quickly realized I had no one with whom I could share what I had seen.

So, I began the school day going through the motions and figuring out the layout and where my classes were located. I remembered that they had a football program. When I went to the office to enquire, I noticed that the football was not round, so I told the administrators in the office that it was not a football. I told them that I thought they had a football team. Some guys were offended, but this led to me learning a new word, 'soccer.'

Canarsie High School was a better school as compared to the zoned school I was supposed to attend. However, there was still a huge culture shock. The environment was a lot more relaxed. I felt as though the students and teachers didn't have any manners. By manners I mean respect of authority and respect for each other students. I quickly learned that being Jamaican meant that you would frequently be targeted. I felt I was honor-bound to defend myself and my country against everybody and anybody who challenged our status.

Speaking of culture shock, the difference between schooling in Jamaica vs America is that in Jamaica, children still wore uniforms in high school. Manners and respect were the norms, and it took a big violation on the part of any person for another to disrespect them. The education is tough and well-rounded. In the U.S., I felt like I had already learned the work that was being presented in American classes at that stage.

When it comes to culture, another point to note is that of racism, which is rampant in the U.S. As a teenager or young adult, sometimes you don't realize that acts against you were motivated or determined by your racial background. It was not until I was in college and started traveling outside of predominantly black neighborhoods that I began to understand the action or inaction of others. Having gained that experience, when I looked back at incidences that took place in high school, I realized that many times adults make decisions based on race.

When white kids committed a crime or were "misbehaved," then in most cases, the white kids received lighter punishment than the black kids had they been just as bad. When it comes to white kids, it is considered that they are just being kids, whereas when black kids mess around, they are considered "troublemakers." However, **the truth was that in most cases, we never caused any trouble nor went looking for it.**

On the other hand, when the white or black American kids tried to bully us, immigrants, by calling students of Carribean descent names or jumping us (ganging up on a group of people), it was often met with a heavy response, be it an individual or a group. Thus, it tells that we were always provoked to be violent and were subsequently always seen as dangerous trouble makers.

My first experience with a person who was an explicit racist was when I was attending State University in Upstate NY. I was racially profiled by campus security while driving into the campus parking lot, and the security guard was driving out. I parked my car and began to gather my things for class. As I began walking away from the car, the same campus police that had been pulling out sped back into the parking lot and demanded that I get back in the car. When I refused, he became irate at my cheeky refusal, called me a nigger, and told me to "get back in the fucking car." I still refused as I felt I had done nothing wrong. He threatened to lock me up, and I said, "Go ahead! I will report you because that's not how you deal with a student." I remember that when I went to file the report, I felt so alone because the whole department (whoever was present at the time) was white, and I also thought this would unnecessarily invite more trouble for me. Another point that made me reconsider reporting the campus security was when my friend and I were trying to expand our lucrative business in town on the campus. This discrimination report would have brought too much attention, so I opted out of reporting the policeman in question.

Racism is deeply connected with bullying. In my culture, being a bully never works because you will eventually have to face the consequences. My only encounter with bullies in high school was when I joined the Canarsie Soccer Team. We had to raise funds to get new uniform and equipment. I was selling boxes of candy and M&Ms. Just before the start of the 2nd period, I sold two bags to two kids. All went well initially; however, just before the class started, they came back to demand a refund claiming that the bags were already open. I refused to be punked, so I told them they were talking bullshit and stated there would be no refunds since the bags were in good condition.

The boys were upset and walked away as class started. I thought nothing of it. As class ended and we headed downstairs amidst a sea of students, someone hit the back of my head. I began to look around as I moved with the rest of the students. I saw the same two boys and realized they were trying to jump me. The fight started in that sea of people. When we finally reached the first floor of the staircase exit, which led us almost to the soccer office, the team realized that I was scuffling with the two boys. The whole team got involved, and huge brawl broke out. Fists were flying from left to right.

One of my friends was an expert at executing perfect flying kicks, so those two boys had it bad. Bookbags were flying everywhere. The students naturally formed a fight circle when fights broke out in school. However, when the Jamaicans fight, everybody runs all over the place, seeking shelter, yet they still want to be able to watch. After that brawl, the two boys who started the fight transferred to another school as they realized they had picked a fight with the wrong guy.

I am glad my soccer buddies stood up for me that day. We showed those two boys what sport really is!

The season I played, the squad was Ruf Cut Razah, Ron, Blacks, Cheeks, Jermain, Baggio, Richie, Famous, Ox, Tallman, and myself. Some other players were in and out of the program or played in a changing era. *Mikey, Brown–Man, Troy Leemax, Ras, Rich, Indian, 50s, Zeff, Sed, ZoZo, and Getmama.* Each is a character and a book in themselves. These were the boys I first encountered when adjusting to life in America. We were young men from all walks of life that looked out for each another and stood up for each other when anybody challenged us. In most cases, we were each other's counsel and advocate when the other was in trouble.

Partly this was one of the reasons why our fights were always so impactful.

Soccer was a pure team sport that tested your wits and endurance. It was amongst my favorite hobbies. It was also my area of interest when applying for high schools. I always felt that soccer was my outlet to cope with the changes occurring in my life. We had a solid team right from the start. We had strong position players that could rotate in different positions to help each other out, and we all loved contact (slide tackle). The 1998-2000 team was not just a team of 11 starters and 7 substitutes. We were made up of the people who tried out and didn't make the squad family. We were made up of friends. Home games were always packed, especially when school friends were involved.

However, games that were played away, i.e., when it's just your squad and travel crew, these games brought us together through some of the sweetest victories and hardest losses. We made it to the quarter-finals, and in my opinion, we were only the second-best team in the school's history just because we didn't win a championship that year. Nonetheless, we all know we were the most bad ass team the school had ever seen.

Talking about fights, there was a long-standing feud in Canarsie high school that started before I was enrolled. I know exactly what started it, but that is not my story to tell. I will only speak with regards to my activity, if at all. Feud is a light word because it was more like a war that went on for years even after the original soccer team members and a couple of school friends had long gone.

The next era still carried on the fight of Jamaicans vs. Haitians. There was an instant fight upon sight, especially if someone got out of line. We also had Haitian friends on the soccer team, but they were not in the war, so they stayed out of sight when shit hit the ceiling. Also, the feud was not only with the Haitians but also with the Football Club. The boys from Brooklyn and whoever was in a gang, whether blood or crips. If someone tried to intimidate us or violate our boundaries, we would "bust their asses." We came to school with knives, then graduated to guns, except that one friend of mine who delivered excellent flying kicks. He always walked with a big stone.

On one occasion, when I showed up at school, I remember seeing metal detectors, and I had my knife tucked in. So, I walked right in and around the metal detectors. However, for some reason, one of the security guards singled me out for a random search. Normally, I would have waited by the gym door at the back for someone to let me in, but my hubris took control. While the guard used his wand to search me down, the security guard (let's call him Larry) was jostling my joint and being aggressive with the wand. My knife became loose now every time he poked the wand. When he reached my ankle, the wand beeped, and he turned to ask me what that was.

I replied, "My dick."

They locked my smart mouth up and took me to the office. At the same time, I saw my friend walking in, and I thought to myself. *I know the stones he has will not cause the alarm to ring.* I was suspended and had to meet the superintendent. When I told the superintendent how I had been assaulted and threatened by the two boys in school while fundraising, which became the reason to keep the knife, they decided to look at my grades. My grades were excellent despite all the class cutting. My participation in school activities, such as the soccer club, was also worthy of notice. Thus, I was allowed to return and complete my high school diploma. When we left the office, I told my mother I was not transferring.

As time went by, the crew started to settle down. Some of us started to work, and some took hustling more seriously while going to school. I had a job at KFC, but we also started throwing parties for our friends and family just to make money and have fun. My friend, Ruffy, started party promotion first. My other friend Lenox and I booked a date for December, so we rented a club, printed flyers, and promoted a party.

As my luck would have it, I met in an accident on my way to the event. Lenox, his cousin, and I were in the back of my pop's car. We got T-boned at the corner of Lenox Avenue and Utica Avenue. My friend went on to the event while I spent the night dealing with the police and a totaled car. The problem was I was not supposed to be driving that late at night using a junior license. Nonetheless, I was in deep shit, and all I could think about was that I hoped the party was packed and I earned a profit. I couldn't care less about myself almost getting killed. I made a profit from that event, and I also got sued by my friend's cousin for the accident. I had no guidance as I should have also sued the person who caused the accident.

So much for being friends!

Having spoken about friends, let's talk about girlfriends. It's just my opinion, but I believe that girls take the term 'relationship' more seriously than boys. As a teenage boy in high school, my relationships were not so serious until they got serious. As per my father, I was young, dumb, and full of cum. I started taking girls seriously just because I didn't want to leave high school as a "virgin," although my virginity was already taken. The talk between my friends was you can't be in school, claim to be a ladies' man without the ladies.

Those numbers don't add up.

Relationships were started just to reach a certain quota before graduation and not to graduate as a "virgin." As a result, the first couple of my relationships in high school were just notches on the belt. Don't get me wrong; I liked the girls. We are all friends to this day. However, when the question was asked, "do you like me?" or, "I don't want to be just another number in your book," the answer was always, "yes" and, "no, I really like you and want to get to know you."

Now the journey had begun because after the 'we like each other confirmation,' a hook-up had to be scheduled. It was easier for some more than others, as my friends had access to their homes easily, I had to coordinate first and ensure mom, dad, and everybody was out of the house and not returning because we cut class, stopped to get a slice of pizza, and I was bringing someone home. I never spoke about my conquest or how it had been planned. But what I did was that when I missed school, my friends noticed.

I would return when school was over, which meant that when everybody was walking out of school in the afternoon, I was walking to school; me and my lady! No question needed to be asked, but it was known that it had happened, and my count was up. This happened a couple of times until I met this wild buck girl from Guyana that caught my eye. I liked her because she didn't care about other people's opinions. She did whatever she wanted to do. She was new to the school, and I think one of my other friends liked her first. But I told him I would try at her to make her my own, and so I did.

We started dating, and it was evident that she was mine. We would go everywhere together. By this time, I was working at KFC while attending high school, and the family had just moved to Queens. Therefore, I had to be extra careful with my hook-up plans, and we would hook up every chance we got. We both would miss school, and either she would sneak me into her father's house, or I would sneak her into my place. Sometimes she would spend the night, and no one would know. Thank God for not sharing rooms anymore. And if Queens was too far, we would hook up at a friend's house.

Things got more complicated when I heard a rumor that she was also sleeping with another friend of mine. I was hurt and upset and confronted her in the wickedest way. I told her since she wanted to fuck my friends, I would invite all of them over, and she could fuck like the whore she is. She never admitted to having sex with my friend, and she didn't fuck the crew, but I broke it off before graduation as I didn't want the drama in my life, going to college, but she told me she was pregnant.

I was shocked.

I was beside myself, knowing that I was about to have my first child straight out of high school.

Despite having such happening my teenage years, I still missed Jamaica, and I tried to visit every chance I could get. Whenever I return to the Island, I always schedule beach trips and hangouts with my friends. I have started to invest in local projects as well. Despite anything and everything, Jamaica will always be my home.

Chapter Four: Bad choices, Good Outcomes?

That first relationship, it can be complicated and tiring. It can also be frustrating and infuriating. The fuss and the fights, the endless bickering nights. Yet, it can also be exhilarating.

Full of passion and energy. Powered by all things wonderful. Glimmering and glistening like magic pixy dust. That is what makes it all worth it in the end.

Relationships aren't easy. No relationship is, be it platonic or romantic. Even the relationship that one shares with their parents is not smooth sailing. That said, every relationship is important in its own right. A serious romance takes precedence over all relationships, as no one is closer to you than your partner. A true partner stands by you through the worst of times and celebrates your successes with you when things are looking up.

One's first serious relationship brings with it many joys and anxieties. The seriousness of the relationship can be measured by the level of commitment of both partners. There is a pertinent need for developing a strong understanding. It is said that couples who understand one another can decipher the meaning behind something as simple as the look in their partner's eyes, the tone of their voice, or even something as minute as a nod of the head.

Understanding stems from spending time together and making a concerted effort to get to know one another. It's not only about sexual bonding but also about psychological and emotional bonding.

Some relationships change the course of one's life. While I value my first love and hold her in high esteem, I never really got the chance to experience my first relationship. Had I been able to do so, the story of my life would have been entirely different.

For both of us, 17 proved to be a ripe age for a relationship. Budding as we were, we bloomed into emotionally and sexually charged lovers.

I first saw her on a school day after soccer practice. My friends and I were meditating. While building a vibe, I saw this girl. She was brown, slim, and short. She had black hair. She seemed shy but full of fun and very feisty. She had a pair of bow legs on her, and when she walked, her hips moved as if she was dancing. I called her style of walking "walk and mhine."

I questioned the guys who that girl was, and one of them answered, "She's Shabba's girl." I kept gazing in her direction. Shabba was in the park, but she didn't approach him. Instead, she hung out with some girls whom we already knew.

I kept observing her for a while but didn't say anything as I was utterly captivated. On one occasion, Shabba and I were hanging out, and she walked by. I asked him if he was with her, and he responded with the 'yes and no, anything is possible' kind of answer. I asked him what's her name and he replied, "Naffie." I told him that I must talk to her.

We finally met several days after I saw her for the first time. We met in the park, and I asked her name as if I didn't know it already. I introduced myself and was just about to ask her where she was from and whom she hung out with. I was asking these questions just to get to know her. I asked her for her number because, in my mind, she just had to be mine. At first, she laughed me off but eventually, I got her number!

In the beginning, the relationship started off fine. When we first started talking and building an understanding, we would share a lot about each other's backgrounds. She told me about her family being mixed Amerindian and Guyanese, about her sisters and mom. We quickly became really close. Being the horny teens we were, we wouldn't miss any chance of having sex. We would cut class after school, cut school after work, and never miss work after practice; you name it! Alone time was prime time! However, the other side of the relationship was not in sync, especially regarding decision-making and planning for the future, something that I completely ignored.

In our own way, we were both serious about the relationship. However, looking back, we were never on the same page in terms of problem-solving. We were just immature and naïve, especially in a world that was new to us.

There were a couple of times over the course of the relationship where we broke up and made up. The first time was the rumor that broke that she had sex with another friend of mine. I was cool if that's how she wanted to live her life. 'Just don't be my girl,' that was what I thought. So, I broke it off. She denied the act of infidelity and wanted to get back together again. I was cool and decided no to. Then I got caught entertaining other females, so she wanted to call the whole thing off. I said, "no problem." One day she came to Queens to pick up some of her things, and we had sex one last time. I cared deeply for her. We had a connection, but Naffie and I didn't get a chance to fall in love. We never made it past the infatuation stage and jumped headlong into the problems stage. Despite everything, we still gave birth to a beautiful baby girl, my firstborn. She conceived our baby after that one last time that we had sex. That make-up and break-up sex is a killer.

I was excited that I was about to be a father, and at the same time, I was scared about what to expect and nervous about what to do. I worked at KFC at the time, earning just about $5-6 per hour. I remember not having any family support, as both her family and mine had refused to stand by us, claiming that we had to take care of our own responsibilities. When I finally told some friends, they sent me some money, about $300. Although it wasn't much, it was something I am grateful for as it helped me figure out who was in my corner.

The birth of my child made me the most anxious and nervous I have ever been. I felt unprepared, to say the least. I had no clue about anything regarding childbirth and child-rearing. I decided that I would be loyal and stick it out. I was going to try to make it work as best as possible. I had just started working my second job as a Direct support staff. I was at least trying to get prepared, so I was hustling. I was preparing to take off by the 9th month and would have built up time. I had already submitted for the vacation, so I was prepared and ready. But this is when I first experienced that one is never ready.

Our baby was due around the first week in May. However, we had an early arrival. The baby was born 8 days after my birthday, April 16th, and I was not in attendance. I got stuck at work for double shifts. Due to the unexpected nature, I could not get time off my job because people at work didn't even believe I was having a child. As far as they knew, I was fresh out of high school. I had to switch shifts with a co-worker to get off and drive 7 hours away to see my newborn baby.

Soon after the birth of our daughter, our relationship ended in the most brutal manner. So, to speak, the quality part of the relationship lasted about one or two years, but when you have a child with someone, that shit is forever.

On my part, I was happy to be a father and would have gone to the end of the world to do what it takes to be a good dad. However, I was not financially stable and couldn't support a family. She wanted to get her life together and decided to move upstate. I was attending school and working at the same time. Somehow, we both wanted to do our own thing and had different views about everything. We were just never on the same page.

Moving forward, the distance was a challenge. I would visit very often, most times spontaneously, up until and even after the birth of our daughter, the relationship had plateaued to the extent that we were still in a rough patch. We were trying to figure out what the next steps were. I would notice things that would not add up and, when questioned, would lead to an argument.

Often, when I would visit the place where they stayed, it would be in disarray, and when I tried to talk about it, an argument would ensue. She would run up the phone and credit card bills and claim not to know about them. I remember one fight we had was because I received a credit card bill for $1500, and when I asked her about it, she said she didn't know where the card was. I got confused because I wondered if she had bought the stuff or not. I reported the card as stolen. The investigative report showed it was for clothes, which blew my mind. The thing was that she enjoyed hanging out instead of getting her shit together. There were a lot of little things that caused many fights.

It goes without saying that we had good times and bad times. My fondest memories are of our carefree moments when we just had fun hanging out all night on the road together or just laid up in bed. On the other hand, bitter memories of the relationship have etched my mind. I was always hurt whenever we didn't see eye to eye about handling difficult times together. Instead, we would be fighting. What hurt the most was when Naffie asked me for money to enroll our daughter in daycare. Instead of sending the money, I went to the school with her and completed the enrollment process, after which I asked to be billed. I left upstate thinking that my daughter would be attending school. As a matter of fact, she communicated with me like it was all taken care of. However, when I enquired with the school, they informed me that the mother never followed up. At this point, I realized that I had to do something. Maybe some men may not care about the decisions made for their children, but my experience forced me to think otherwise.

The relationship definitely became more and more complicated. The primary reason for this was that during her pregnancy, and even after that, the person I started a relationship with, the one I was attracted to, whom I cared for... she wasn't the same person anymore. This led to arguments and confusion, which made the relationship much more stressful.

Eventually, we drew the relationship to a close. We discussed and mutually decided that I would take care of our baby girl. I'd give her a good education and a good home. So, although we were separated, we had a mutual relationship based on the trust that I would raise our daughter well. I took responsibility from that point onward and tried to figure it out and be the best parent I could be.

If there is one thing about Naffie that I feel I didn't value enough was the fact that she never restricted my access to our child in any way or form. I never truly appreciated or valued this about her. I was always able to take my baby if she required anything. Finally, when I offered to take care of our baby on a permanent basis, she did not hesitate to trust me. She knew that I was thinking in the best interest of our baby and allowed me to make all the necessary decisions for our baby's upbringing.

Once I had custody, she would come to meet our baby as often as she could, but the distance and travel time of about 6-7 hours made things quite difficult, especially in terms of coordinating her visits.

Despite all the difficulties and challenges I have faced, I have no regrets about any of my relationships. I learned a lot, and I am a very stubborn person. I never allowed myself to think about what would have happened had I walked another path. I handled the moment that was in front of me.

I bore the fruit of this relationship; my daughter NaSandra Malessa Simone Bent. She gave me purpose; she gave me a reason to put things together. Because I had my first child early, I wanted things early. I wanted a car, and I wanted a house. I wanted to ensure we were financially set. I was always hustling because I had that responsibility at an early age.

NaSandra is the light of my eyes, with her bubbly personality and free-spirited yet principled nature. What's more, today, at the age of 18, she's the mother to a beautiful boy. That makes me a grandad!

Chapter Five: Stepping into the Grave

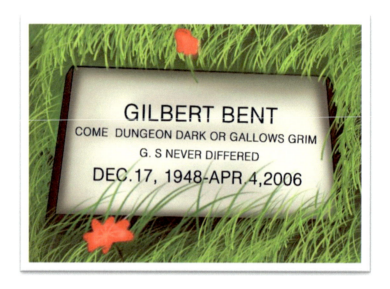

GILBERT BENT
COME DUNGEON DARK OR GALLOWS GRIM
G. S NEVER DIFFERED
DEC.17, 1948-APR.4,2006

To the Faithful Departed

My father passed away on April 4, 2006, at age 57. It was a surreal moment for me. I did not know how he passed because a proper autopsy was never completed. On his death certificate, the cause of death was documented as siriasis of the liver and heart failure. However, his death was by no means of natural causes. I clearly remember that he had a clean bill of health when a physical was completed a few months before his death.

It was even surreal discovering how he passed; he passed away in his office slumped over his desk. I was 20 years old at the time, and you could imagine it was heartbreaking. Unfortunately for me, this is something I can articulate because you never know how someone's death will affect you. The most prominent feeling that I can point to is that I probably shut down and never dealt with my feelings surrounding his death. Another reason was that I was living in New York when he passed, and I had to travel to Jamaica, West Indies, for his funeral.

Funeral for the Faithful Departed

I have crystal clear memories of his funeral service, and it was incredible. He had a traditional service for an officer that died on the job. He received tributes from the Police Federation and Harewood Past Student Association. Mr. Samuel Morgan gave his remembrance speech; he was the Deputy Superintendent of Police at the time. The services took place at his favorite church, which was The Church of St. Mary The Virgin, and he was buried at Dovecot Memorial Park. Thankfully, he had his entire family with him, including children, grandchildren, brothers, and cousins. His friends from the police were also present for his final rites.

Despite the paid respects, the atmosphere at the funeral was tragic and chaotic since he passed away so unexpectedly. I could not hold back my tears when I was there. I was surprised and upset and found it quite unbelievable. I was distraught because the last conversation I had with him, not long before then, was an argument regarding providing my older sister with assistance. Even though feeling that way, I still didn't process what that loss would mean to me or how hurt I would feel in the days coming up to his burial and after. Knowing that he would not be around to witness my achievements was devastating. I kept aching for another chance to talk to him and see him smile back at me, but I knew that would not happen. We take people for granted and only feel their importance when they leave us. The song "Don't know what you got till it's gone" by 1980s heavy metal band Cinderella echoes my sentiments well.

At the same time, the atmosphere also fit well with my feelings as it was somber and surreal. It looked as if Mother Nature was crying along with the rest of the mourners and me. The best part of the funeral was that everyone who knew him or was ever impacted by him showed up to show their support. At funerals, you go through all phases of emotion and frustration when dealing with planning and attending events.

One unreal experience for a young man was dealing with family members attempting to collect my father's outstanding debts. At an early age, I had to contend with contributing to burying my father and settling his debts. This was the most bittersweet rite of passage that had to be done.

I was thankful for the fact that he had a lot of love and support from people who knew him, respected him, and appreciated him for the person he was. Since you can never please everyone, you would have haters, and as they say, "haters gonna hate." The same was the case because he had haters for the same reason he had those who loved him. The haters showed their disregard for him through their actions because, as you know, actions speak louder than words.

I was hurt but had to be strong for the rest of my family. This was quite a challenge for me. I had to hold back my feelings to show support to my loved ones and ensure each event went as coordinated. Funerals in the Caribbean work differently from funerals in the United States. These include a nine-night wake, memorial services, and the final burial. I remained strong as I could until that final part.

As my father's casket was lowered into the ground and covered with dirt, I felt my tipping point. I broke down as soon as the graves men stuck the placeholder to mark the site in the ground. This was the final farewell, and it struck a massive emotional chord with me.

My Father's Eyes

That moment when it was all over has resonated with me to this day. I still think about all the best times I had with my father. I can say that our relationship was quite cordial. I remember how my father was principled in every sense of the word. He was a strict disciplinarian, but I did not have to face such rigidity. He had afforded me more leeway.

He was not the type to be present for school functions, but he would take me on weekend trips to hunt, go to the country to visit the properties, and visit my grandmother. He was the type of father to be respected. It was not until a brief instance before he passed, on one of my return trips to Jamaica, that we bonded as friends. He taught me life skills that I appreciate to this day. This is why I regret my last conversation with him. When I had such a great relationship with him, I feel I could have made our last conversation better than it was. We had a disagreement about what makes a supportive father.

If wishes came true….

That being said, father, he never showed affection or emotion much, but if you are his friend, you will know when he is in one of his moods. He had a different gear when it came to the ladies. His demeanor was of a gentleman, and his verbiage went from broken to proper. On the flip side, he had zero tolerance for bullshit, and if he felt offended or disrespected, he was quick in his decision-making to address it.

This is a true example of his principles.

Regarding his work ethic, my father was dedicated to his job. He cared about his mother a lot. He loved hunting, traveling the countryside, and drinking. He could never stand thieves and liars. Like every man, he was not perfect. He had strengths and weaknesses. His strengths included loyalty to his friends, which I feel was his best quality. He enjoyed cricket just like most of us and loved retro music. Those were the golden years, according to him. By retro, I would say Bob Marley, the Beatles, Jimi Hendrix, and Elvis. His weakness was his inability to control his anger, which contributed to his hot temper.

My father had not studied higher education because he went straight into the police academy after graduating high school. He later became a Sergeant for the police department. I am inspired by his level of commitment to his career and pursuance of professional growth. He also held very high moral standards as promotions were passed over him several times in his career due to his principles and political motivations. Perhaps my father did not know that he would pass away the way he did, so he left no will but a lot of colorful and beautiful memories behind.

While you may assume I would be grieving for days or even months after his passing, time, responsibilities, and professional commitments would not allow me the chance to mourn for him. Therefore, time healed my pain. Looking back at the time of his passing, I could not put it into words and bring myself to understand the loss of a loved one despite it being a horrible experience.

Echoes from the Past

I have countless childhood memories of my father. One of my fondest memories was of the time when I traveled to the countryside with him on weekends. It was not the time spent with him but how he would take me into the rural country and give back to the needy and deserving. This instilled a love for philanthropy in me, seeing how my father reached out to those in need.

Another fond memory of my father was the time I spent in high school with him. I can never forget the wonderful Sunday afternoons cooking with him in the house. He would wake up every day at 5 am, clean his car, water his plants, and get ready for work. Other than that, he would watch cricket, cheer for the Windies, and listen to retro classics.

For the Love of Cricket

When it comes to cricket, he was a massive fan and would always talk about classic West Indies moments, such as the two cricket World Cup victories in 1975 and 1979. For those unaware, these two editions of the tournament were the inaugural ones. Our boys reached the final in 1983 against India but lost to the South Asian Giants.

Cricket World Cup tournaments take place every four years. Even though there are more formats of the "gentleman's game," such as T20, the spirit of the game is pretty much intact. My father was a fan of Sir Vivian Richards, Richie Richardson, Courtney Walsh, Curtly Ambrose, and former World Cup-winning captain Clive Lloyd. Cricket is a beautiful game. Although it is not as popular as soccer (or football as I call it), it still has a solid global following thanks to the advent of franchise cricket like the Indian Premier League (IPL), which is similar to the soccer leagues in Europe function.

Careless Memories

There is so much to write about my father that can fill an entire book, and I feel honored to dedicate a chapter to him. After he left my family and me, I felt a part of me had been taken from me, and it did haunt me despite the fact I eventually moved on when I went back to the real world. I realized that the moments you lead in life determine the legacy you will leave in death. Whatever we do in life becomes our legacy, and people will remember us only for what we did when we were alive, good or bad. That is how I remember my father and honor his legacy.

That being said, I have recently begun the grieving process by taking care of my responsibilities regarding his estate and accepting that I now own it. Apart from the love he bestowed on me, his estate is the only thing I have of him that I will take care of until I join him in the heavens.

I have realized that grieving is a process and a time when a person experiences emotions about how certain events impacted that person's life. There are five stages of grief: 1) denial, 2) anger, 3) bargaining, 4) depression, and 5) acceptance. I have gone through all these stages, and by writing this book, I can say that I have reached the acceptance stage. I have come to terms with his passing and am at peace with the fact that our loved ones will not stay with us forever, but their memories and love will remain in our hearts. They also will have a second life there; I can feel my father now lives inside me, and I shall cherish him forever. Grieving is normal because it is an emotional response to coping and moving on from tragic life events and trauma.

Thank you so much for reliving my father's memories with me. Please, take care of your loved ones—whether it is your children or parents—because we do not know how long they will stay with us. Cherish them in both life and death because the latter is a reality we all must face. It humbles us and allows us to spend our days wisely in this world, as my father did. He served the people as a policeman and will forever be remembered for his services.

I have always loved him, and I urge you to love your parents and give them a great big hug if they are alive and near you. They must know how much you love them because you do not want to regret it like I did when I did not have the best last moments with him. I pray your folks live long, happy lives; when they leave you, they leave you with the fondest memories.

As I close this chapter and before you move to the next page, I have left you with this incredible and profound quote by him:

"Come dungeon dark or gallows grim; I will never differ."

Chapter Six: Baby Girl's
Popping Out of the Lap

"When life gives you lemons, make lots of lemonade!"

I was only 19 years old when I had my first child! You may find it quite surprising because it is usually unheard of to have a child at such a young age. I named her NaSandra Malessa Simone Bent, and she has always been special to me as she was born three weeks before her due date. She was born in the same month I was born, that is April and we share the same Arian sign.

I find it very interesting that everything, good or bad, happy or tragic, happened to me in April, whether it was my father's death, my birth, or Sandra's birth. Her birthday is April 16, 2001. I was scared out of my wits because 19 is too young of an age to be a father. This happened right after high school, and her mother was still pregnant. Not many people knew other than a few friends of mine.

Growing Pains

It was a very difficult time for me. My girlfriend got thrown out of her house close to her delivery, so I had to take care of her and provide her with a home. When I spoke with my parents, my stepfather was very much against a child coming into their house. It was a horrifying situation. In those days, I was not allowed to work full-time due to my work permit, but thankfully, the manager allowed me full-time and overtime work because of my situation.

This new work regime changed a lot of things for me. I had to give up a lot of things I loved to do, like having to give up playing soccer. I would forget to attend team practice after school and work at KFC till closing. It became a mundane and robotic routine. School, work, and repeat every single day. I earned $7.50 an hour, and it seemed like the money never added up. I could never earn enough to take care of my girlfriend and eventual mother of my daughter.

I reached out to my friends and family because we were couch surfing from one place to another and were getting tired of being soccer balls going from one goalpost to another. My friends and family loaned us up to $400, but it was not enough for an apartment. We ended up staying with one of my girlfriend's cousins in Rochester. We had to get the baby delivered so she could figure out what to do.

As you know, my baby daughter came three weeks early. I immediately took on the role of a father and changed jobs, thanks to my girlfriend's connections. It was very hard as I had to pull double shifts to take care of my daughter. I had to work and be on time to see my daughter's birth in Rochester. I could not believe my eyes when I saw her for the first time. I just knew my life's goal was to be there for her and protect her. It changed my mindset at a very young age.

Things were getting challenging. I had to shuffle between two cities between work and being there for my daughter and her mother. I gave her whatever I could, like my credit card and a phone, and we were facing a tough time. Both my girlfriend and I could not see each other. The relationship went from bad to worse.

I agreed to take care of our daughter for six months while her mother got on her feet. I decided to send my daughter to Jamaica under the care of my sister. I had not seen my baby for six months, and her mother was missing her, too. Eventually, I brought our daughter back, and we decided to co-parent, but that did not happen. I filed for her custody and eventually became her mother and father. I became a single father at a very young age because I knew I could best take care of her.

It was not easy to bring her back and file for custody, but I managed. It took around six to nine months to get my daughter enrolled in school, and that started my journey into a full-time single father. I had to do everything, like get her proper medical care and get her immunizations up to date. I had to make sure that I was listed as her parent and guardian in all paperwork.

While it was an initial struggle, I eventually gave my daughter a family. I started living with another high school girlfriend, and her mother was very supportive of our little family. My girlfriend eventually had a daughter so I became a father of two girls. Then, we had a son together. I was so glad my firstborn now had siblings, parents and a family. We were a proper family. My firstborn went with me everywhere because I wanted her to be an integral part of my life. We eventually got our house, and I had married my girlfriend.

Life is unpredictable, and as time went by, my wife and I grew apart and eventually divorced. I became a single father again, and I wanted to ensure my baby daughter, who had grown up, got through high school. When she was in junior high, she saw that my marital relationship had hit the rocks. I did not give up and continued caring for Sandra.

Gangs and Sandra

I went through high school and did everything I could to graduate. I also took care of a teenage pregnant girl and raised a daughter by myself, but I did not join a gang. I found out my daughter was part of gangs as I tracked her phone and found out things I never thought were possible.

I thought she was on a track team, but her teammates were gang members. Her track coach informed me that she never attended training. I did not have a wonderful encounter with her gang, but thanks to my street connections, I got the lowdown on them. I was working at an agency far from my street roots, but I knew that a gang was never something I would join.

Sandra was not happy and later complained to her high school that I was an abusive father. It seemed like my baby wanted to have nothing to do with me because her new family was her gang whom she felt at home with. I once got a call for a domestic disturbance incident at my house, and when I reached home, there was an ACS investigation taking place. I was in the middle of this cold war between myself and my daughter's gang. I was getting promoted and now had to face legal charges.

Sandra would take every opportunity to be away from home because she never wanted to be around me. I was busy with meetings, and she would skip school. My deepest and darkest fears were about to come true as history was apparently repeating itself.

She's Havin' a Baby!

My daughter became pregnant as a high school teenager, and I could not believe it at all. Her mother was also pregnant in her teenage years, and now my daughter was having a baby. My world had turned upside down. Up to this time, I had faced so much trauma in life. I had to deal with the loss of my father and the challenges of raising a daughter as a single father. I had to endure her joining a gang and now becoming a teenage mother-to-be herself.

But in the same sense, I was in the middle of so much turmoil. I couldn't celebrate it like that because having a kid as a teenager is not the worst thing in the world. But just the whole disrespect, the lies and the trauma that she told, and running away and not being present, and having to go to court back and forth was tumultuous for me to handle. When the authorities hit me with the ACS case, they took her out of the home and placed her back with her mother, whom she'd never lived with all her life.

Sandra could have lived a normal life as a healthy high school teenager. However, she chose not to and fell victim to her own demons. I shed the most tears at this point in my life because I'm like, she didn't understand how much sacrifice or how much shit I took. I had to make sure that she was okay. I cried so much that there was a point where I stopped driving to work because she would run away so much. I would tell my friends about her wearable hood to just look out for her, So I used to walk and look out for her. And wherever I saw a group of teenage girls, I would try to see if she was there, but I never, I've never, you know.

Our relationship really went through a strain of struggle. It was hard for me to reconcile all of that and see how maladaptive she was being. I used to have conversations with her like, I'm trying to help you out. Every move I made was to try to take care of my family and to try to make sure my kids were living a good life.

I had to deal with my legal troubles and headed back and forth to court. I was treated like a criminal, but the justice system here is all about innocent until proven guilty. It impacted my life and my work. I became very depressed. Sandra would go on the witness stand and tell lies, and I had to deal with all that nonsense. I took care of her the best I could, and she turned her back on me. She was lying out of her teeth while pregnant. I ended up being very strong. I knew I had to advocate for myself and my family's rights.

Things went full circle when her baby was born, and I showed up at the hospital to see my grandson.

The child would grow in trauma, and I had to take charge of his life and rescue my daughter, his mother. I had to treat her like an adult because times had changed. She became a mother out of her own choice at the age she wanted to be. I dedicated my life to helping them regardless of my feelings and the hurt and betrayal she had caused me. It was a matter of time when Sandra's mother and I reconciled, and she apologized for how she had hurt me in the past.

Looking back at it, I believe everything happened for a reason. And you know, everything, for the most part, has begun to come full circle. So I'm glad I'm still in a position to help and support her, but then she definitely popped out of the lab real quick. I wasn't able to guide her out like I wanted to, like every parent dreamed of. Maybe it's my own selfishness, but I didn't get a chance to teach her how to drive or take on her first job interview.

We did not get to see her graduate high school or get to take her on a college trip, to go look at college schools. I've never gotten a chance to do any of that. And that, too, is still kind of emotional for me because I'm like, I work so hard to be able to give you this. But because of how you view your life when you just had a traumatic reaction, and you just blew it all to smithereens, you just dropped the bomb in, in the thing, so.

So I die.

I feel like I didn't get a chance to come full circle and be that parent for her. Those were some of the things that I had missed, you know, losing my father early in life, but I'm grateful enough that we still had the opportunity to communicate. And she blessed us with a grandson, and as young as I was, I became a grandfather at 38.

That's the story of my daughter. My baby girl popped out of her mother's lap, and now she's on her own at 18 years old, trying to find herself with a two-year-old son.

Chapter Seven: The Other Half

Sooner than later, I realized my relationship with wife was not working. She caused some of my daughter's pain, and my daughter blamed me for it because I put her in that situation. It was tough for me. So, I had to make a choice.

Should I stay in a relationship that didn't make me happy and wasn't going well? My first child was suffering because of this. Or should I leave, get a divorce, and start over?

It was a hard decision for me.

I was young and going through this for the first time, and I didn't have anyone to talk to for advice. I kept away from the people I usually ask for help because I didn't want to hear their opinions about the relationship. I had already made up my mind and isolated myself from everyone. I didn't know how to handle the situation.

Sometimes, I had to go to work even though I was unhappy and things were not going well. I was also finishing my bachelor's degree while getting a divorce. This should have been a happy time for me, but I was also feeling sad because my personal and family life was not going as it should. It was a challenging and hopeless situation.

I remember going to work and feeling like I was not doing well in some areas. My daughter was not doing well, and my relationship with the mother of my children was falling apart. So, I started doing things that were not good for me.

I never wanted to see myself like that because I was still dealing with my pain. I was trying to recover from a harrowing experience and struggling with a relationship that had fallen apart. I mostly blamed myself, thinking I had messed up and was wrong for not being able to take care of my family or guide my wife properly. It was tough for me to go through this change.

I tried to act happy and do well whenever I went to work. But sometimes, I felt sad and down, especially when it was time to go home. When my divorce was happening, there were moments when I didn't want to be at home. Even when I visited my kids, I sometimes felt the same way. I often left and distracted myself by drinking or spending time with others.

To lessen the pain, I dated multiple women. I was still married, and I was seeing other women. I remember when I was out with someone else, and my soon-to-be ex-wife, Beryl, saw my car parked somewhere. I was at a hotel with another woman, and she moved my car because she had a spare key. Before I went home with my then-girlfriend, I told her not to move my car if she saw it parked on the street.

I think that's when I realized I had hit a point where things couldn't get much worse. So, I decided to move out and start my life over. Starting fresh is scary because you're basically starting from the beginning. You have to figure out how to sit down with your kids and tell them that things will be different from now on. It was really hard to explain to them that Mom and Dad were getting a divorce. I thought it was better for them to hear it from me rather than hear incorrect stories or lies about why this was happening.

I clarified that our decision to separate had nothing to do with them because we loved them very much. I promised them I would still be there for them, and we would do our best to ensure they had everything they needed. In my mind, I was committed to that promise, and I believed their mom was too. But I quickly learned that when people are upset, they don't always act the same way.

The situation between my ex-wife and me got worse and more stressful. Whenever I tried to see my kids, she would send them away. I had to keep going back and forth, trying to be there for my daughter, especially because she was about to start high school. Going through this change and trying to be a source of support was really hard. I can only hope I did a good job, but honestly, I'm not sure. What I do know is that it was a very tough, challenging situation.

Alas, I started to distance myself from certain people in my life. I became short-tempered, easily agitated, and filled with anger.

***

When I was 32 and going through a big change in my life, I met someone amazing. She saw I cared a lot about the people I looked after, especially because I worked with individuals with developmental disabilities. I was really committed to how I managed my programs and trained the staff to be patient and help those with disabilities learn new things or keep up their skills.

From her point of view, she saw that I had a special quality that, at the time, I didn't realize in myself. She noticed I was struggling in my bad relationship, and we stayed friends. It turned out she was also going through similar problems with her partner.

We had lots of talks, and I shared information about my life and things that happened in the past. She gave her thoughts, and it all came down to one important thing: my old relationship taught me a valuable lesson. I had tried to make a relationship work out of something never meant to be. It didn't turn out the way I had hoped, and we grew apart in different directions.

That's when I realized I needed to be honest about what I wanted and what would make me happy. I also needed to be clear about what I expected, especially when starting any new relationship. I felt that from now on, I needed to be completely open about who I am. Being upfront and truthful would let the other person decide if they were willing to deal with everything.

I decided that in any future relationship, I would be honest about who I am and what's important to me. The other person needs to know my true self, my values, and the things that are important to me. I started remembering what I stand for— being a good person who cares about family and a loving, reliable individual. Talking about these things helped me understand my value because someone else saw it.

Eventually, the coworker and I became really good friends, formed a strong connection, and, over time, we started a romantic relationship.

We started working closely together, and I began teaching her what I knew about my job. I worked as a manager at one place and also overnight at another. It just so happened that the overnight job was going to take over the place where I was a manager.

I took the lead in teaching my staff how to be a manager. I shared all my knowledge about the industry, different ways of managing supervising skills, and why taking action right away is important when dealing with people's lives. I stressed the importance of addressing problems immediately and ensuring follow-up actions were done quickly, documenting, and filing. In simple terms, I trained her in everything I knew.

But I later chose not to keep the management job because it didn't make sense for me to stay. Because of the company's policy, I couldn't work overnight with the union and be a manager simultaneously. I decided to switch to a different agency and become a manager there. I would help a director who knew I was good at managing. My friend—who is now my wife—and a few other staff members decided to come with me. They followed me to the new place and the new job. I kept on teaching my friend, even after we moved.

I began by giving her a job as a medical coordinator, and she did really well in that role. After that, I promoted her to an assistant manager job. Later on, she moved into a job as a home care liaison and did a great job there, too. Around the same time, I applied for a better job and got promoted to become an administrator.

As my career improved, my eldest daughter came to live with us. This happened in our first year as a couple. At the same time, my now wife was also doing well in the same line of work. She was climbing up the ladder in different roles, using the knowledge I shared to do well.

During this time, we had to deal with my daughter's difficult behavior in high school. My current partner was there to help me through it. Our relationship became even stronger as we went through this big change in our lives together. It was the first time I felt I had someone to lean on. I'm not the type to ask for help, but she knew what I needed and did things without me saying anything.

This is the kind of person I've needed all along, I thought.

Luckily, she felt the same way about me, and we both realized we could have a great future together. Then, we had our son, who is my fifth child. Later, she got pregnant again, and now we have our daughter, who is almost ten months old. She is my sixth child and my wife's second child. So now I have a total of six kids.

***

I had to go through many legal cases, like divorce, child support fights over who gets to keep the kids, and even cases with ACS where they said I did something wrong but didn't offer any help. It was tough, but my wife's support made it easier.

Then, things got even more complicated when COVID-19 came, and the court system stopped working. Some of those cases are ongoing today, and some haven't been solved yet. Even with all this, I feel more confident in fighting these battles because I know I did the right things and can be held responsible for my actions. I also know that some things people say about me aren't true.

Many of the cases are still not figured out, and many of my follow-up actions are ongoing. We're still working on them. When ACS came to our house to check on things, I had to take the lead because their visits were mainly for my young son, who wasn't the one having problems and didn't need help. They were supposed to make sure that I got the right services and check on my son's safety and my eldest daughter's well-being. I had to be proactive and make sure the caseworkers did their job.

When I insisted they do their job properly, sometimes they saw me as an angry Black man. I told them it was important to do their duties because my child was still having maladaptive issues and not getting the help she needed. These are problems I've had to deal with.

It was like a big surprise in the story of my life. I didn't think my wife and I would get along so well, talk to each other so clearly, help, get each other's unique qualities and habits, and even stand up for each other sometimes. I never thought I'd meet someone I could teach and show my skills to, only to see them perfect them and teach me new stuff. We've worked together to create a life, which was a surprise but good.

I believe that God has indeed seen my struggles and chose to bless me with happiness and true love.

For me, this is a wonderful thing. We can go on trips whenever we want, and our families really like each other. Together, we're creating a life full of love and happiness for our kids and families. I never thought I'd be this happy in a relationship. It feels like I have everything I need, and any other accomplishments in the future will be a bonus.

I even have a house in Jamaica where I can relax on the beach and live freely. I also own land where I can grow things and live a simple life. I have a loving family, and the most important thing to me is being with my kids and positively impacting their lives. I want to teach them to take responsibility for their actions and help them when life gets tough. I work hard to understand their feelings and to support them on their journey. I'm always learning and growing, and life's journey keeps going.

Life has been a big adventure, and even though I'm still pretty young, I've been through a lot. I'm thankful for the chance to breathe, and now I can concentrate on understanding the different parts of life, getting into coding, and helping those who need it. My main priority is taking care of my family and protecting my kids' emotional well-being, even if it means risking my life for them.

I feel wealthy because I have God, my loved ones, a reliable wife, and the happiness of spending time with all my kids. Anything else that comes my way is like a bonus, and I'm thankful for it. I thank God every day. I'm so happy that I want to help others as much as possible. I don't advise everyone, but if you need help, I'll do my best to help you. That's how I want to live the rest of my life.

Chapter Eight: See, I Told You

For me, success is being able to help others, supporting your children or family's dreams and goals; having a level of respect and love for helping somebody. Success, in my opinion, is not solely about money or status but about making a positive impact on others. That's what brings me joy! Sometimes, people may not remember or value the impact I've made, but I do it for my reasons. Over the years, my definition of success has evolved as I've learned to balance giving to others while focusing on my goals and dreams. It's about finding that equilibrium to avoid getting too absorbed in one aspect of life, whether career or personal and ensuring time for self-care and individual goals.

I aim to be recognized as someone who consistently pours into people, particularly those working with developmentally or intellectually disabled individuals, advocating for those who can't do so themselves. Regarding my life goals, I aspire to build my own company, ensuring a heritage for my kids and loved ones. I want to take steps to achieve these goals, even amid life's busyness. Although managing accounts and training staff may dominate day-to-day activities, I try to find time to expand and focus on my dreams.

Over the years, I have faced significant challenges and obstacles in my journey toward what I define as personal success. My past relationships had been difficult, shaping how people perceived me. In my past relationship, I believed I was with someone who loved and valued me and wanted to grow together, but that was not the case. I took responsibility for investing time, having kids, and eventually getting divorced. Finding someone new made me realize the importance of being valued for who I am.

However, obstacles still arise, where there has been a need to be mindful and give assurance. Not only that, I also faced challenges in my relationship with my oldest daughter. But even after going through bad relationships and encountering supervisors or employers who didn't know how to respect and deal with people, I'm happy as I learned and understood something new with each hardship. These experiences contributed to my personal development, strengthening my resolve and progress toward my goals.

It's challenging to precisely measure my progress since life is 'lifeing' (something I like to say) continually moving forward, and I haven't yet found the courage to let go of the day-to-day grind to focus solely on my goals. As long as I continue working toward it, that's good enough. My long-term goal is for whatever company I'm running to be competitive in its industry. Until my peers recognize me as a competitor, it remains a work in progress.

There was a time when I was working multiple jobs, going to school, and dealing with my first marriage, that eventually led to divorce. When I thought this could be it, I managed during the day and worked overnights, budgeting money in a daytime management job, and attended school in between. It was hectic for me. Despite the difficulties, I knew that I had to prioritize myself to achieve a higher degree and provide for my family. Learning to put myself first became crucial because, without personal well-being, I couldn't effectively lead or look after anyone.

I knew I had to stick it out, working multiple jobs while finishing my college career and ensuring I graduated. This degree was essential for the next step in my career. That process shaped my confidence, teaching me that I could persevere and succeed no matter what happened in life. It was a defining moment for me.

Getting my degree played a significant role in shaping my character. It made me resilient—no matter the hurdles, I had the drive and motivation to succeed. That experience kept me motivated and focused. There were times I had to put personal goals on hold to prioritize family needs. I couldn't take away from my family to build a business at that moment;

we were going through a lot, and I needed to work to handle day-to-day situations, pay bills, and ensure everyone's well-being. However, in the back of my mind, I always knew I had many ideas, and if I could find a way to implement them, I believed it would ultimately take care of my family.

To this day, some of those ideas remain on the back burner, but I know I just need time to piece together the puzzles. The more I work toward financial freedom and success, the more I can dedicate time to my personal goals. That's how I stay focused, drawing from those experiences and defining moments that have shaped me.

***

While working the overnight shift as staff at a company, I managed for different agencies outside during the day. Despite being a staff member, I applied for the position of administrator, which would be an important jump from being a staff member to supervising those who managed me. I remember applying while juggling work and school and attending the interview while I was going through a divorce. My current/now wife—who was a friend at the time—encouraged me to go for it, saying they might not have hired someone yet. I decided to take her advice and went back for the interview. I was confident as I had experience in the field. I knew all the answers asked during the interview, which impressed the interviewer, and I got the job.

At that time, two administrators were needed to oversee the entire borough where I worked. Coincidentally, my co-administrator was going through pregnancy just before the onset of COVID-19. Once the pandemic hit, she went on maternity leave. I ran the entire borough department, including the residential department, with only one administrator and a few other staff members.

The COVID-19 pandemic posed challenges for everyone, including the Vice President. Despite the impact it had on my life, I appreciate the experience and the guidance I received from her and the executive board members, who were also navigating the new challenges brought about by the pandemic. I remember dealing with the loss of individuals both among my staff—who lost family members—and the people we were caring for.

As a supervisor, I had to lead my team through a challenging time during the pandemic when they were fearful for their lives. Coming to work meant facing the risk of a life-threatening infectious disease. On the other hand, not working jeopardized their livelihoods and the lives of the people we support. It was a tough position, but I showed up to work every day that I could.

I remember the entire management team pulling together, showing up to work every day, not working from home like most companies. We checked in on our sites, believing that this was achievable. As a young man who not so long ago was being supervised, it came full circle. Now, I was supervising and being one of the point persons in the bureau, admin at Brooklyn, leading the team through the pandemic and taking directions from the head office, state, and other authorities.

I guided my team, emphasizing that they could keep themselves safe by following procedures and protocols, maintaining cleanliness, and observing safe distances. I ensured that we stayed on top of the changes during the pandemic, implementing various mandates and providing necessary PPE to staff. I monitored the proper use of it and adherence to COVID mandates, guiding staff on how to don and remove protective gear safely. We organized vaccination drives to protect our population, liaising with pharmacies through my head office. During these drives, I ensured my borough was organized and ready, guaranteeing both staff and the people we supported were vaccinated. The pandemic presented challenges, but adaptation was crucial.

It was a life-changing experience, especially experiencing the pandemic at its peak. It gave me a new appreciation for life's fragility and brevity. Having contracted COVID several times, though it didn't impact me as severely, witnessing my now wife's struggle, despite following all protocols, made it clear how serious the virus could be. Her oxygen saturation was critically low, and she was struggling. I had to contact one of my friends, the VP of Nursing at the time. He advised that it was dangerous for her to stay at home another night. I activated EMS, and it took about three hours with medical services in the ambulance before her oxygen levels normalized enough for them to transport her to the hospital. Thankfully, she fought and gradually recovered her health.

***

Soon, the company decided to hire new executives and make some changes in positions. Unfortunately, the new executives weren't too thrilled with my efforts. This left me in a depressed state initially. However, I quickly realized that it wasn't my issue. I couldn't let someone else's perception of me define who I am. I snapped out of it and refocused on my work.

I went back and forth with upper administration and the new people they brought in for a long time. However, I came to realize that everything happened for a reason. I realized my goals and dreams that 'I couldn't let myself become too complacent with the day-to-day challenges.' I had a conversation with my wife and decided to leave the job. While she was sad, knowing my love for the field—the people we care for and my team—I felt it wasn't worth fighting for a company that didn't reciprocate the same level of commitment as I did. So, I resigned from that position, and my team and the borough office organized a celebration for me.

This meant the world to me because those people were my team, and I did my best for them. They sent me off like I was retiring, giving me a golden farewell. I really appreciated it, and their gratitude helped affirm that I was doing the right thing.

My mother was there, and she got to see the impact I made. She knew that I climbed the corporate ladder and had risen to a specific level, understanding how challenging it was in the field as she worked in a similar field. She witnessed how much my team appreciated me, which served as a catalyst. Even before that, she started coming around when she saw my hard work, college graduation, and return to school. We've had a challenging relationship, but it felt like it came full circle. I used to think my work ethic and attitude came from my father, but upon reflection, I realize it largely came from my mother.

My mother believed in hard work, maintaining high standards, representing oneself well, and working diligently, trusting that everything would eventually fall into place. This belief aligned with my experiences and contributed to my success. I was confident in every decision, including stepping away from the job and recognizing the importance of knowing when to leave and pursue my path. My mother's support was instrumental in influencing my pursuit of success.

Now, I realize that a relationship requires effort from both parties, and it takes two people to make it work. Even if you feel like you're doing everything or being unfairly blamed for mistakes, the other party may not reflect on their errors.

When I could rebuild my family and see my children again, my mother's words, "See, I told you things would work out," provided a sense of approval. It reinforced the idea that doing the right things, supporting your children, and being truthful in your actions will ultimately work in your favor. This experience significantly impacted my perspective and life choices.

From that moment on, I always expressed my feelings and treated people respectfully and honestly, just as I wanted to be treated. I've lived my life according to these principles, unwavering since then. This wisdom from my mother guides me to be truthful, work hard, and prioritize taking care of my children, knowing they will come back to support me.

Chapter Nine: Boy, You Can Cry/Smoothing the Edges

I want people to understand the message that life goes in cycles. Life absolutely has an ebb and flow to it. Once you have life, you have a chance. A chance to correct mistakes, a chance to undo trauma, a chance to face fears, and an opportunity to work on things. So, I think the primary message is to pay attention, don't be disheartened by incidents, and see the silver lining along with opportunities that present themselves.

The book is titled "Boy, Men Don't Cry," and a couple of things inspire it, but the overall theme is that you'll cry sometimes. There are a couple of parts in the book where I've been broken down and brought to tears because I felt unable to act. Everything I did at that time seemed to turn out wrong, and all my actions sometimes yielded terrible results, no matter how well-intentioned.

But that was, and it brought me to tears. However, I had to realize that it was only at that moment. I had to pull myself together, fight through it, understand that I am a good person and I am committed to doing what is right. Regardless of the situation, I am determined to hold myself in high regard, operate on the right track, and believe that everything will ultimately work out in my favor, no matter how long it takes.

We don't know the time. We can't predict when hurt will come our way, but everything happens for a reason. It's a fact that there will be moments when you will cry. It's the societal expectation that men are supposed to be tough, that they should suck it up and keep moving. This is unrealistic because men have emotions. Humans, in general, both men and women, experience emotions too. If you lock up those emotions and don't give them any attention, you are bound to have a lot of trauma.

It's important to know that you must deal with your emotions. You have to accept them, process them, and let them out. Understand why you feel the way you do. You must self-reflect and confront those emotions. You must challenge yourself to find a way to work through them for better results. Being a man and saying, "Oh, you gotta toughen up and don't deal with emotions or don't feel any emotions," is ridiculous. Expecting a man to be tough and devoid emotions is unrealistic, even for someone like myself, who considered myself tough and believed I had no feelings.

Yeah, I did cry sometimes, and that was okay because it was important for me, an essential part of releasing how I felt, facing fear, acknowledging life's struggles, and dealing with them. It's crucial for me and, I would say, for other men to accept the fact that they will encounter struggles and challenges, be it in relationships, at work, or in the face of racism.

You will face struggles and challenges, and being comfortable with that is essential. You may not always respond appropriately initially, but having time to reflect, process your emotions, and autocorrect is valuable. Being alive always means you have a chance to change your circumstances.

Not everybody will accept you for who you are or vibrate on the same frequency as you. It's okay if people don't see things like you for their reasons. The key is to be aware that you have the opportunity to change and grow.

You have to be comfortable in yourself, knowing that you will do the right thing, and strive to better yourself and the circumstances of those around you. There are two key points I want my readers to understand truly. First, that life goes in ebbs and flows; it's cyclical. My father would say, "Come dungeons, dark, or gallows grim, I will never differ," meaning stand firm in your resolve to be a good person. Second, remember that, as the saying goes, for every dark cloud, there's a silver lining. In every situation, there is always a positive aspect.

I have faced challenges, and at times, I've been tempted to address things most negatively and viciously possible. However, I've listened to that inner spirit within me each time, telling me that such an approach is inappropriate. In cases of misunderstanding, it's crucial to seek understanding first and handle people how you would like to be treated.

Every time I've followed that advice, putting out the energy I want to receive, it has either changed someone's opinion of me (if they perceived me negatively) or altered the situation's outcome.

So, that's the lesson I have learned that has helped shape how I approach things moving forward. I put out what I want to receive into the world, whether the situation is good, bad, ugly, or indifferent. I consistently project what I want to see, which always comes back to me. Even if people don't immediately understand it, they recognize that I've given them a chance, and I've put into the world what I want in return.

If I can offer advice that has been instrumental in my personal and professional journey, it would be to put out what you want to return to you. If you project positivity, positivity will come back; if you project negativity, negativity will come back. Becoming a young father placed me on a path to be mindful of my actions.

In Jamaica, they say, "Whatever you do, if it doesn't come back to you, it's gonna come back to your kids." Karma.

So, being a father and now a grandfather, seeing that my bloodline is extending, knowing that I have given life and that life is being shared abundantly, it has certainly impacted how I move forward. I am mindful of my actions because I don't want negative karma or cosmic energy to affect my children and grandchildren. I often pray that the father's sins don't become the children's sins.

That's why I deal with things differently now, taking a moment to think before reacting explosively, as I used to in the past. I used to be impulsive and ask questions later, but now I approach things more surgically. In the past, I drank alcohol and smoked weed to cope with my trauma, but I quickly realized that wasn't truly me. I don't want anything to control me; I prefer to control myself as much as possible. Therefore, I avoid doing things I know I'm not in control of.

The second way I used to cope with trauma was by not dealing with it. However, I eventually realized that this approach became difficult as I had a lot of pent-up anger, aggression, and emotions. So, I came to understand that I had to process, deal with, and comprehend the impact of trauma on me. I learned to release that energy into the world positively, accepting the things I could change about myself and leaving alone those aspects that I couldn't, especially when it comes to changing people. You can't force others to see you in a certain way if they don't want to, and you can't make them have respect for you.

I've recognized these two things and understood that I need to face traumas head-on, be honest about how they affect me, and find ways to move forward. I've abandoned putting blinders on and just moving forward without addressing issues. Now, I address problems, deal with them, and move on. I make sure people know how I feel, striving to treat others how I want to be treated—open and honest. Even if there are times when I feel it's not the right moment to deal with an issue, I approach it with caution. Nevertheless, I am committed to addressing situations and people in a manner that aligns with being open and honest.

When I lost my father, I didn't grieve him the way I would have liked to. The pain and the fear of loss still lingers, and I'm particularly apprehensive about losing loved ones. However, I recognize that it's a natural part of life and must face it. So, I'm still working on and growing in that regard.

Instead of focusing on the negative, be grateful and look at why it happened. Evaluate yourself, understand what's happening, and figure out how to dissect and change yourself to respond differently, altering the outlook or scenario in that situation.

I hope my journey through life and my experience in writing this book will inspire others to overcome challenges and pursue their dreams.

Regarding role models or inspirational figures who have influenced my life, values, and actions, I would say it combines my father's steadfast belief in truth and justice and his work ethic, never selling oneself short. It's also influenced by my mother's dedication to hard work and efforts to be a good person.

Make sure you put good energy into life. I don't have many inspirational figures, as I view people as people, acknowledging that everyone has made mistakes and has skeletons in their closets. So, I look to those who are real about their situations, authentic in their actions, and how they deal with things.

If I had to pick two role models or inspirational figures whose books I've read and whose lives I admire, it would be Bob Marley and Nelson Mandela. I believe they lived and walked the talk, self-sacrificing, sticking to their beliefs, and letting that guide and carry them through. I would say they are the ones who not only inspire young men facing difficulties and striving for success but also inspire me to leave a legacy for my sons and grandsons. I want them to know and expect that for a young black man in America, life isn't going to be easy; it just isn't.

If you're going to deal with relationships, the work field, being social in life, and dealing with people in general, it will not be easy. People won't always treat you as you want, as everyone has their views and opinions. Therefore, you must be able to take your experiences with a grain of salt, analyze yourself, and always maintain a positive outlook.

Stand firm in your beliefs and recognize that you always have options. That's the lesson I want them to learn, the legacy

I hope to leave through my experiences, lessons, and the challenges I've faced in life. I want them to understand that they are strong individuals but must recognize that life will not be easy. They will have to keep fighting, pushing forward, and never giving up.

I hope everybody can apply these insights and live better lives because I have made mistakes in how I dealt with relationships and trauma. However, it is crucial to realize that you must face, process, and dissect them. You need to understand what they mean for you as an individual and determine how you will conquer and overcome them. Consider how you will relate to people who may be adversaries or competition, as these situations reveal aspects about yourself, you may have never known. Responding positively and keeping your head up is essential. Keep fighting.

Family Pictures

About the Author

Gilbert Stephen Bent (Jr.) hails from the tropics on the golden island of Jamaica, where he spent his early teen years. By his mid-teens, he migrated to the United States with his family, where he gained a unique experience of what it means to be a man of Caribbean/African descent, a family man, and a model father. Gilbert Bent Jr. holds a bachelor's degree in management and finance and is a successful businessman.

In his book, Gilbert delineates the struggles, hardships, perseverance, and successes that made him the man he is today. The first half of his book was written on his plethora of visits to his homeland, where he would visit the golden beaches and crystal blue seaside, which propelled his inspiration to write. The latter half of his book was created from his frosty crystal window as he recalls the wintry moments of his life that catapulted him from boyhood into manhood. His story digs deep into the recesses of his being and recalls his fight to maintain his sense of self and identity.

Made in the USA
Columbia, SC
18 April 2025